For all my wonderful friends and family, especially my Ma and Pa

col·lec·tive noun \kə-**lek**-tiv naůn\ *noun* : a term that describes a group of individuals (e.g., troop, gaggle, flock).

Animals have varied social lives, family systems, and living situations. Some animals live together in large groups of thousands. Others prefer to be alone but like to know that neighbors are nearby, and some animals are very particular about the other animals they spend time with. But no matter how many are in a group or which animal is in charge, each species lives in a unique social order. Maybe animals aren't too different from people, actually.

A Tower of Giraffes

Animals in Groups

Anna Wright

i⌢i Charlesbridge

A Gaggle of Geese

When geese are together on the ground, they are called
a gaggle. When they fly, often in a V shape, the group
is known as a skein. The bold geese at the back honk to
encourage those in front to move quickly. *Honk*! *Honk*!

A Colony of Koalas

Most koalas live on their own, so there isn't an official word for them in a group. Since they don't live too far from other koalas in the bush, their overlapping territories are called colonies or populations.

A Scurry of Squirrels

Squeaky squirrels hang out in groups called scurries to protect one another. Ground squirrels make a whistling noise to warn their scurry about approaching danger.

A Herd of Elephants

Girls only here! Female elephants, or cows, live in a group of about ten called a herd or memory. Each cow pitches in to find food and care for the babies, called calves. The males, or bulls, usually live on their own.

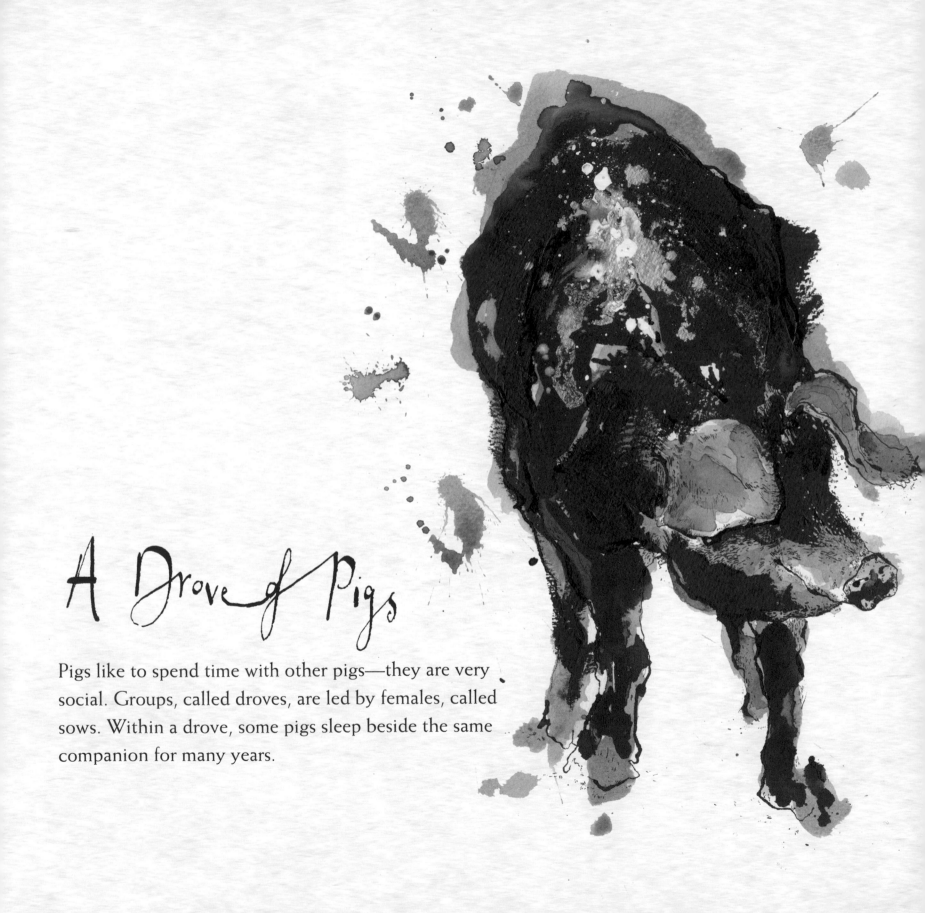

A Drove of Pigs

Pigs like to spend time with other pigs—they are very social. Groups, called droves, are led by females, called sows. Within a drove, some pigs sleep beside the same companion for many years.

A Flock of Sheep

Sheep are shy and stay in a group called a flock to keep safe. If danger comes too close, the sheep run swiftly in a wild and woolly whirlwind to get away.

A Parcel of Penguins

Sink or swim, penguins love being together! These social birds swim and fish in groups called parcels. Some types of penguins spend time on sunny shores in breeding places called rookeries, which can include thousands of penguins.

A Mischief of mice

Furry families of mice live together in a group called a mischief, usually led by a male mouse. Male and female mice help care for the babies together.

A Prickle of hedgehogs

Most hedgehogs like to spend time alone, but sometimes they meet up in a group called a prickle or an array. They are primarily nocturnal, or active at night. Females bred in captivity tend to spend time together and will seek out another hedgehog.

A Flamboyance of Flamingos

Flamingos are highly sociable and live in large colonies of about three hundred birds called flamboyances or stands. Sometimes thousands of them meet up. These fancy feathered friends work together to make theatrical displays by posing like ballerinas and marching in time to impress other birds in the colony.

A Romp of Otters

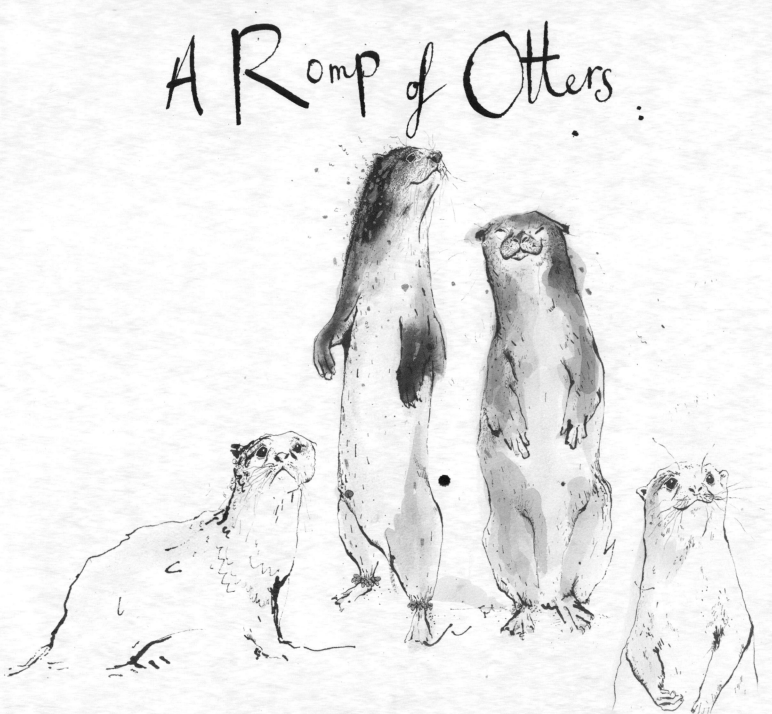

Sea otters float in groups known as romps, not only when sleeping but also while eating and resting. A romp can range from two to several hundred animals. As they float around, the otters hold paws to stay together.

A Parliament of Owls

These wise birds like to work alone. Barn owls live in a group called a parliament only when they are protecting their nests and their fluffy little chicks.

A Troop of Monkeys

Monkeys live together in large social groups, much as humans do. In a group called a troop, they help one another to find food and stay safe. But they don't like newcomers! A monkey from an outside troop is usually not welcome.

A Caravan of Camels

Camels live in groups of up to fifteen animals called caravans. They like to gather at springs and oases in the desert. These noble humpbacked animals are not very territorial and cross paths with other caravans without problems.

A Tower of Giraffes

Female giraffes live together in a group called a tower and are very selective about their companions. They make friends and avoid the giraffes they don't get along with. Male giraffes tend to live on their own.

An Ostentation of Peacocks

Peacocks are social and often live in a group with one male and many females, called an ostentation, a muster, or a pride. Males have blue-green feathers with "eyespots," which they spread to attract females. The birds nest on the ground but stay safe in trees at night, and they have a very loud call.

2015 First US edition
Copyright © 2015 by Anna Wright
All rights reserved, including the right of reproduction in whole or in part in any form. Charlesbridge and colophon are registered trademarks of Charlesbridge Publishing, Inc.

Published by Charlesbridge
85 Main Street, Watertown, MA 02472
(617) 926-0329 • www.charlesbridge.com

First published in the UK in 2015 by words & pictures, an imprint of Quarto Publishing Plc, The Old Brewery, 6 Blundell Street, London N7 9BH

Illustrations done in ink and watercolor, then collaged
    with fabric and feathers
Display type hand drawn by Anna Wright
Text type set in Weiss Std by Adobe
Color separations by XY Digital, London
Printed by C&C Offset Printing Co. Ltd. in Shenzhen,
    Guangdong, China
US edition designed by Whitney Leader-Picone

Library of Congress Cataloging-in-Publication Data
Wright, Anna, 1984– author, illustrator.
    A tower of giraffes: animals in groups / by Anna Wright.—
First US edition.
        pages cm
    "First published in the UK in 2015 by words & pictures,
an imprint of Quarto Publishing."
    ISBN 978-1-58089-707-5 (reinforced for library use)
    ISBN 978-1-60734-919-8 (ebook)
    ISBN 978-1-60734-920-4 (ebook pdf)
1. Animals—Juvenile literature. 2. Animals—Nomenclature
(Popular)—Juvenile literature. 3. English language—Collective
nouns—Juvenile literature. I. Title.
QL49.W89 2015
590.14—dc23   2014029098

Printed in China
(hc) 10 9 8 7 6 5 4 3 2 1